P9-CPW-083

CARTOGRAPH

To Auntie,

i hope you enjoy

these new journeys.

[signature]

CARTOGRAPHY

CARA-LYN MORGAN

thistledown press

©Cara-Lyn Morgan, 2017
All rights reserved

No part of this publication may be reproduced or transmitted in any form or by
any means, graphic, electronic or mechanical, including photocopying, recording,
or any information storage and retrieval system, without permission in writing
from the publisher or a licence from The Canadian Copyright Licensing Agency
(Access Copyright). For an Access Copyright licence, visit www.accesscopyright.
ca or call toll free to 1-800-893-5777.

Thistledown Press Ltd.
410 2nd Avenue North
Saskatoon, Saskatchewan, S7K 2C3
www.thistledownpress.com

Library and Archives Canada Cataloguing in Publication
Morgan, Cara-Lyn, author
Cartograph / Cara-Lyn Morgan.
Poems.
ISBN 978-1-77187-151-8 (softcover)
I. Title.
PS8626.O7438C37 2017   C811'.6   C2017-905323-X

Cover and book design by Jackie Forrie
Printed and bound in Canada

Notes: stanza one, line one in "We are the Train" is from Sylvia Plath's poem
"Blue Moles"

Thistledown Press gratefully acknowledges the financial assistance of the Canada
Council for the Arts, the Saskatchewan Arts Board, and the Government of
Canada for its publishing program.

Acknowledgements

Some of the poems that appear in this collection have appeared in their earlier forms in *Descant, Room, Qwerty, Brick, Fiddlehead, The Dalhousie Review* and other literary journals in Canada. The poem "mîscacakânis" was chosen for inclusion in Turnstone Press Ltd's *Best Canadian Poetry in English, 2015*. Marsii to the small presses, you keep art happening in this country.

To David Arawapit and the six other children who walked from Whapmagootsui to the steps of Parliament in January, the month of bitter cold, I want you to know that your footsteps were heard. Keep walking.

A humble and heartfelt thank you to The Banff School of the Arts Creative Writing Experience for granting me the time and space to bring this manuscript to its completion. To the poets I met there, thank you for your guidance and support. Especially, and always, thank you to Lorna Crozier who remains at once the toughest editor and also the kindest.

To the early readers of my work, June Halliday and t m taylor, I love you both.

To Seán Virgo, marsii for muscling these poems in a way that delighted and challenged me. And for that word you returned to me, which my ancestors could not.

Thank you especially to the Forh family, who nursed me well during the most humbling and painful time of my life. I thank you for your couch, your television, your food, your patience, and your love.

And again, to the ghosts who settle in and press their stories to my sleeping skin. I hope I have honoured your voices.

And to my love. Sean, you have given me a new kind of poetry and a whole new name.

CONTENTS

kâ-itâpisinahkâtêk ôma askiy — map

how beautiful, this place

quiet and weak and still

love, selfishly

for Letitia and Amelia, who have also found their way

Why do poets think
They can change the world?
The only life I can save
Is my own.
— Sherman Alexie

kâ-itâpisinahkâtêk ôma askiy — map

East — the old church

Kieran presses his palm flat
on the belfry glass, boylike,
facing east. This boy,
so like our uncle, he watches
the landscape wide
and wild. Duck Lake,
our people have prayed here.

East is yellow, the colour
the cones of the eye see
above all others. East, the place

of sunlight, the warm
skin of springtime which blisters and peels
then emerges pink and sore
and new. Kieran steps back
from the window, leaving a smudge
from his broad hand.

*Cousin, are we the last
to come here?*

South — the lake

The place of red, untilled clay beneath
rough sand, curls of paint on old barns left
to ruin. We root ourselves here, clung
to a past. Lake Manitou, the boys swim

silent and shrinking in the low
chops. We girls stay with the babies
as our mothers did, palming
wet sand into buckets. This beach
has narrowed since
our childhood. Back then it yawned
wide from the reedy banks to lap
the salty current.

The boys emerge and we huff, relieved
as they doggishly shake off the lake, whoop
and wave. We watch as they
suss out the old medicine
wheel, brambled
and ancient as the grass.

They walk the stoney path
we once did, when our legs
were strong and new.

North — the sky

This is the place
where the grandmothers sleep. We turn
our faces skyward, the quiet
reach of wakening. It is the afternoon
spectacle of sundogs, how we stood
in our doorways and pulled
our blankets tight. North,

white strip of absence,
sky against earth. The custodial
nature of winter, how it arrives
at night silent
and cautious, meeting
our boot prints, the delicate
press of a fox's paw. How dark
a place this is in winter.

West — the shore

A stretch of sky and water, thin white seams
of blue rocks. West, the place I fled
to in my wildhood, where our country ends
and the ocean eats it. Lorna calls this place
the spirit line, where all the ancestral
families live. Here,
a place of stone, and water. Blue,

a word both song and colour. Steel guitar,
upright bass. How grown I felt
under the stage lights, my back
to a boy who hugged
the polished bass, pressed
his chest hard on the womanly
curves and played
into her with a delightful
violence. Blue

the careful
heads of chicory, how they bob
on the asphalt, their spiny
shadows on the pale. Upward
thrust of crocus in winter, forcing
the season's end with a shock
of colour. How the moon
becomes blue
when the month runs
long, carrying in its wake
chaos, mischief, sorrow.

how beautiful, this place

Returning to

this tilled soil where our family's dead are eaten
with the wheat, drunk by the slow tendrils
of spotted lilies. This length of coast,
of cedar and alder and red arbutus, slouching.

After that,
the Rockies, pressing feet
to their blade-sharp crags. The jagged
ridge of the badlands, a place of rock
and violet sky. Spiral
of vulture, warm Chinook.

And at last, the edge
of lé prairie. The place
where the grandmothers,
my grandfather, and Uncle Patrick walk
still in elk-skin shoes. Here, the gold
and blue swallows dart
among bending foxtails.

May this braid of sage burn us home.

homecoming, humboldt

Did I go? Did I walk
the intended road, collecting
the past like stones in my pocket? Have I grown
from a girl who felt the push

of the iris in spring and learned
to let her oldest bones lead her. I have
returned again

and again, to this place which knows
the lung, which frosts and needles
the marrow in winter, crisp
as a boot track in snow.

It is more than the skin
of my cheeks in winter. More
than the blood-thieving ticks
in spring. Will I walk

until the bones of my feet
clip on these pale sidewalks?

Lumsden

fat rain. beyond the brazen fields,
thunder.

the cows muddle up the hillock, breaking
their fast on soaked clover

old bells call
heavy from their necks.

we come to the place
where the dead

petal open, offer up
the wet cavities of their hearts, fisting

blood, their cage of bone
pulling back, pulling.

hoar frost, funambulist

Trinity Bellwoods

A ring of filthy men around a thin blanket, yellowed playing cards
tossed in like coins between them. The baby, Layla, hangs from
the infant swing, arms limp, legs kicking. A row of new teeth
eats at the frigid air as she screams, delighted. Now and again
she spies her own feet and squeals, clapping her mittens. A boy
on a slack-line pulls himself up then falls, blushing. His sneakers
squeak on the wire. Jagged lace of hoar frost on windows. The
trees have shed their heavy coats. We pocket mittened hands,
stealing back heat from denim thighs. Across the park the Santa
Claus parade lumbers down a snowless street. *Funambulist*, I
say to my sister, and she repeats it, smiling. The mouldy funk
of leaves silent beneath our boots. My sister has gone pink and
lovely with this cold, her hair tamed by the dry air. We warm
our mouths with the steam from our coffee. She slows the baby's
swing suddenly, as if caught by surprise. "It's winter," she says to
the sharpened air.

kick, kick, kick

Grand Central Station, Midday

Brass, brass, and below me
a man plays his electric piano, someone
whistles and the crowd shakes
the rain off like a pack of dogs. A black haired
woman hugs her child, palming
his soppy tears and chuckling

as he wails. I see
the many ways we wear
each other: in the rigid palm, mashed
into collars, sucked tight in the weave
of our cuffs. Licking back

like the coyote pup, or those orphaned
elephants, how the calfs wander
the wilderness, trumpeting distress, calling out
to their slaughtered mothers, how they become
sleepless, longing through the night
for the thrum of her

massive side. How our grief
makes animals out of us, licking back,
our faces flung skyward, mouths
slacked, teeth exposed in a bright moon.

We too trumpet
our loss into the cheeks
of one another, spreading
sweat and liquid like hard

honey whiskey, bodies
trembling with breath, so eager
so eager
so eager our thirst.

we started with a walk

for David Kawapit

Whapmagoostui, the place of the beluga
a day fifty below freezing
where ocular fluid chokes
on the lashes, blood
shrinks and steams, and the teeth
hang slick and loose. You began
in the month of bitter cold. Heavy

snowshoes and denim darkened
to the knees with ice, seven children
setting out through bush
and snowbright paths
shielding split lips with woollen scarves
toques ducked forward against
the wind and daggered snow.

You walked through a month
of pelting ice, eyes on the oldest maps
of this place. Walking
the ancient pathways to show us all
that you remember.

Idle,
they called you.

riverbed

Walk to the place where the trees drop crabapples, sweet-looking
and bitter. Cross the street to the park where my dad flew his
purple kite one September, then packed. Once, on the hill there
I trampled a ground wasps' nest and was swarmed. My dad, afraid
of insects, pulled me out too late. That night my grandmother
drew me an oatmeal bath, then slept with me and the nightmares.
Walk on. Beyond the pathway where we rode our bikes to the art
gallery on Saturdays. Beyond a bluff where the sun filters through
poplar snow. There, the hiccup of owls spitting up mouse
bones, the scritch of chipmunks on spruce bough. There, all
things unknown are dappled and brown. There, the place of the
freckled. The path smells of dry leaves and droppings. Be still
despite the mosquitoes. Follow the sound of the river to where
the bank is dull and crooked, and the water copper-cold in spite of
summer. Many times I washed my feet here, when I was a child.

Put your face to the current, and drink.

human and strange

Octave of dew, falling
from birch leaf to supple
ground, silk webbing
the roots of cypress trees.

At night
the owl cries across the lake.
At dusk

a mother loon, skimming
the surface
like a skipped stone, her nestlings

slipping one by one from
her spots to the water
and back again. She watches

us, turns her black eye backward
as she glides. Beneath the water
her feet pedal, the frenzied
calm of motherhood.

Shorelines

*Michael Belmore at The Museum of the American Indian, 2006
New York City*

how cold it stays
in this heated room. the artist
has pounded roughly
the outline
of his country into pocked sheets
of copper. lakes and cracked

rivers, a thumbed-out cautious
prairie edged in the sharp
upsweep of mountains
borders determined once
not by men but
water, its patient cutting

back clay and soil, rock. all the ways
that time eats, suckling
roots, the slow chipping
down of coulee walls.

how human to have been here,
how foolish.

16

skin
pale and erupting
at its pores. Hair,
always greasy, curling out
the wrong way. She spends

the morning leant across
from her reflection
a heated sewing needle
in her hand, rubbing alcohol
mingling with the Pine Sol clean.

She presses the needle's blackened point
into a lumped face, willing
a rush of pain and yellow white
puss. When she sees blood,
she wipes the bathroom mirror,
she swabs the wounded skin, witch
hazel and tea tree oil. Wolfs

her teeth at herself, crowded, mis-spaced.
Folds too-thick lips
around their ragged edge. Retreats
for a full body view to measure
the hand-width of her thigh, shakes it
just to see. From the downstairs

bathroom, animal
sounds: her beautiful sister
vomiting.

We are the train

1

They're out of the dark's ragbag, these two
Skulking and lingering, drawn down from the lit sidewalk.
Thumbs an easy curl in cut-fingered gloves, black pens clutched —
Waiting for a tourist to protest. The small town
Within me flutters in my chest, I am outnumbered
In this flickered light, on the Jersey-bound
Platform between tracks A and B:
A tilted taking in of me over curved noses,
Lips kissed out like snarled dogs.

Underground, there is no sky, no starry sanity.
Only this merciless dripping, the upper pipes
The skitter of mice across still rails. One boy
fingers his crotch, brown hand clutching
Baggy denim. The other flicks his eyes at me, taps
His friend's down-swelled shoulder. I shift
my handbag on my stiffened arm, pretend to read posters.
They nod to each other; I have no one to tell.
Wordless, they draw up their fur-trimmed hoods, scrawl
On the cracked wall, and are gone, black tags scarring.

2

Please stand back from the closing doors.
A cattle shuffle of wool coats and hats. Lurch, jostle.
Get us home now, get me home. To an armchair, a meal.
Sharp black marks above the curved window, tags
Unreadable in this white white light —
Samo says jumps out and I smile. Charlie Parker
Charlie Parker. I feel closer to Basquiat down here.
Down here, we ghost ourselves alone.

A mauling of gloved hands parting
A path through business suits, baby strollers,
Arms leaping through closing doors, pressing in,
The force of bodies through bodies. The loosening
Of ties, dropping of eyes, thoughts of slipping
Thick slippers on swelled feet; chain-clank and shuffle
The journey homebound. We scan black walls, blurred brick,
 Skirts or pairs of shoes, music piped to our eardrums
To drown out the words outside. Down here,
We are the train.

My father makes Bake

dripping tap water
from his brown fingers into the dough, forming
a flat, warm mound, then piercing it
with the prongs of a large fork.

He slices strawberry and apple
into the buljol, bringing
to mind his eldest brother who lies voiceless
in a home in Trinidad, withering
from some elder's disease. Remarks, again
how my granny would be horrified
at his addition of the fruit. *Uncle's recipe*, he says. The island
years-removed from his cadence. My father
doesn't weep

when he chops the onion and the kitchen
smells of salt cod and hot sauce. Here,
among the autumn frost, with his black
and careful hands, he knows he is making
bannock in the old way. These days,

my father does not eat green iguana. Here,
he sucks the meat from rabbit bones

the place of deer
for Tim and Helen

This evening, on route
to Manitou, the lake
my teacher knows
so well. He tells me

the water there
is healing. Medicine men
carried it in vials
to tend to the ill. I can
only hope it cures
the haunts of the body
and, especially,
the mind. Behind us

Mt. Douglas is a dark
and rustling hulk. He calls it
by its first name,
its old tongue name which means
he says, the place of deer.

On this island, I have
always been a settler, my tongue
thick with wine
and soil, and I can not speak.

Behind us,
the half-wild house cat
and the slow moving fawns
scuffle through dropped leaves.

reunion
Watrous

The family tree. We twig out names
on white posters taped
to the cookhouse wall. Each night
we sing in the dead
saying the old prayers, calling
their names. The grandparents
tap photos of their younger selves, blushing,
recalling the ferocity of youth.

They ask me, constantly,
which of my sisters I am, accusing
us of growing to look too much
alike. We press our thumbs
to our chests and say our names,
Alanna, Jacqueline, Cara, as they shake their heads
and then forget.

The cousins we played with
as children come to us as adults, strangers
to my useless memory which carries
facts and dates, but never names
never faces. Still, we clink the slender necks
of our bottles together, passing
beer caps off to the younger ones
who pin them to their tee-shirts
with the aluminum tabs from their cokes. The uncles
round up their own aged cousins
to play kick the can on the gravel driveway.

All of us, children.

mîscacakânis
Watrous, 2012

you are my yearling. I have brought you here
to give to you the prairie, a place to be human

and small and at mercy. In the evenings, you sleep
and I breathe a scatter of Michif into the soles

of your feet. You are *mîscacakânis*
my little coyote, running along the scattered flatland

with your arms above your head. Screaming, casting
your long shadow out on the narrow railway line.

We taught you to swim in Lake Manitou, the weightless
surf, then washed the salt from our skin

in the outdoor shower. In the morning
I braided sweetgrass in your hair and then you ran

barefoot and unafraid, shaking the dew
from yellow canola. You drift off in the afternoon

smelling of soil and sweat, sunlight and crop.
I have brought you here

to give to you the only thing
there is. May you be wild,

a girl-pup, mine
from long ago.

Georgian Bay

morning: wayward unpetaling
of red lilies after thunder

crouch of voices
through a tent wall, how the canvas

inhales with the lungs.
the grey gull claws its beak, pebbled

eye on the tide. flash
of minnow. lightning, lightning bugs.

soon the seagull will return
to feast. dragonflies carve

the water's surface, swallowing
blood-drunk mosquitoes.

here, with the living, I am
a flung spark at the fireside.

Killbear Provincial Park
Ontario

he brought her here to still
the bleating, be quiet
and unneeded. here
where the birches limb
across a green moss
of cypress. she wanders

an early morning
path while he snores
heavily, drunkenly
from the truck's bed.

she comes
upon two yearling
doe who pause
as she enters their space
and stare, ears alert.

a rustling sound
as the canopy sheds
the weight of last
night's rain. then,

hunger. the deer
return to their twigged
breakfast and she
to her walk, thinking

of the grand ecdysis
of birch, unpeeling
itself pink. she came
to this place to quiet
the screech, still

her fingernails from breaking
her skin. how silent
he kissed her, hands
moving slowly, then
releasing.

leaving her
goose-fleshed.

how beautiful, this place
Vancouver Island

I

A merle of blackbirds
eyes me from the electric wire
they pull these poems
from restless fingers.

behind me
an old man kicks his empty beer can.

the flock scatters, noiseless.

II

early morning,
a piper sails by
on a very small boat. his tune
ghosts
the quiet harbour.

on board, a single
drummer beats out
above tufts of low cloud.

how beautiful,
this place.

Georgian Bay (II)

Blue,
fanned crest, tipped wing, the jay
its sudden flare of bold
in the mizzled green. Cypress
and towered birch
cast crooked shadows while rain pools
on the slackened plastic of our tents.

We string wide tarps tree to tree, map out
our village, unlace heavy boots and press
the wet wool of our socks to the spitting fire's edge.
Cedar branches pop sap into beads, as we drink

the last shiraz and drift off,
nylon tombed. Outside, near empty
beer bottles clink. The raccoons,
breaking our silence
sucking.

homecoming, lake manitou

These are my mother's cousins. Grandparents now, they crowd
the picnic table singing folk songs from memory. They are the
children my mother played with. Tonight she drinks wine from
a plastic tumbler and tells me about their weddings, how well
the family two-stepped, how they'd come home in the mornings
bruised, shoeless and exhausted. These nights, I am overcome.
These are the oldest prayers I know. Yesterday,

I watched my uncle kicking stones on the street where they spent
their childhood years. Really, nothing changes here. The eye
remains full of the yawning sky, the fields human and desolate.
The farmers lament that the soya beans creep north with each
warm summer, and that the private abattoirs where we buy our
salted meats are closing down one by one.

We all left here, so long ago.

quiet and weak and still

These days, the trees

Atop the power line, a hawk.
Beneath his perch,
a mouse. These days
the trees bend

left, leaves stretching
for roots, shadows
on fields of prostrate
dandelion. These days

my eyes search the wild
daisies, black-eyed-susans
I used to pull, greedy
to thread through my hair.

They never stayed
linked and I wept
when I saw I had killed
them, scattering

petals across the grass,
dead stems on cut
lawns. I watch the hunt,
cheering first mouse,
then hawk.

minutien

deltoid, mossed bone, perpetually wet and sunlit
beneath a stretch of fat and skin. Deltoid, the beautiful
front. Space of resting palms, house of the precarious
clavicle where the boys took pucks in winter
and arrived at the rink sullen and slung
for the season, skates hanging
by their laces, blades gone to rust.

the deep fascia of the human shoulder, muscles roped and bound
to the bridge of clavicle, acromion, spine
of the scapula, scapulars, the little plaques which hang
beneath the shirt like a stage pass. Removed
each evening from the soft hair of his chest, kissed
passionately then held above the dark
nightstand, rope pooled around the Christ's
handsome face. Deltoid, the place my lover left

his teeth marks, dashed crescents of blue and purple,
mouths opened in terror, eight of them crawling from my silent
throat, down the left blade. He moaned, biting into
the hot blood below. I did not cry out. Blue
to yellow then curves of dark green, faded
altogether until my lover, as well, was gone. Trapezius,
pectoral major, cartography of the back, the neck,
the wired fibres tough as coir, the mats

where we scrape the mud from our winter boots
in the barn's doorway. How easily torn, stretched, wickedly
tender, brachii, dorsum, the place of the head
a glance over the hump of the shoulder, lane change
the sound of one's name in a crowd, here
the baby sleeps sweaty between the rigid jaw bone
and humeri. Unlike the hip, the shoulder does not hold

emotion, it holds the coat, the thick braids
of scarves in autumn. In summer, it sheds
its skin and pinks itself infant and new. A man
smelling my shampoo in an embrace, a draped towel.

The acupuncturist thumbs out the nerves and presses
his needles in, one by one. Feels out the spaces
of each spinal bone, the fisted and torn
muscles in relentless spasm. He would release
the bad memories in the meat of the shoulders
swording into each place of injury, willing
it calm. He counts aloud each needle, *relax*

relax. Deltoid,
a pinned moth
on a velvet board.

Monarch-shaped, a delicate beast

with wings wide and flat, it rests on the rigid cartilage of the
throat. That place where a lover breathes a soft and humid kiss.
Thyroid. My sister paints her fingernails a vibrant pink then
leaves for the hospital. I burn the good sage, the plants I pulled
from the hillside in Lumsden, as the cancer is cut from her body.
Thyroid, a creature no one considers until their jeans don't fit. I
speak to the grandmothers as she receives a straight and bloody
cut. The anesthetic makes her nauseous, weakened not by cancer
but calcium as it leaks from her bones. Tumour, we have paid our
cancer debt and yet the palm seems always outstretched. Drowsy,
she asks me to braid her hair and I do, fingering my way through
dried vomit and curls. The last time I did this, ten years ago

the night before her wedding.

vernacular of injury

This language of blood
and muscle and bone, housed
on the walls of the examination room
charts of human
injury, worrisome, promising,
chronic, benign. Roadways

of artery, the in the out,
each strain in the shoulder
and back, I can not learn
their proper names. The doctor

enters, pressing the curtain
aside. Palms her manicured hand
into broken muscles, and clucks
as though it were I who slammed the brakes
too hard and whipped myself
into this elderly state. She asks how

long since the accident, mistaking that it helps
to talk. I look at the posters instead, silent.

I feel like screaming
all the time.

quiet and weak and still

I have been made
a stranger to these bones, this skin,
the screeching, ragged muscles. Mine,
a body I have slept
in over thirty years. Strange,
to have had muscles which fanned
and rivered and bridged the blood, and
had always quietly done the job
they were meant to do. And yet, again
here I am naked

on a slab, an acupuncturist
pressing twenty needles into the wrecked
knots of my back and shoulders, twisted
neck and the soft dent at the back
of my knees. Twisting. Releasing
the *qi*, he says, "bad energy." What little
I recall of the accident leaking
up, dissipating like bubbles
above the evening wash. He uncovers

my weariest darks,
places young and exposed, palmed
and pressed and struck from behind again
and again. This, yes strange
path of my healing,
separate. Quiet
and weak and still.

amitriptyline

nights like these
I take my medicine
and the fairy
goes back in her jar

haunt

for my father

As a girl, I dreaded
to be called here. You, framed
darkly against the bay window, empty
street. Heavy tenor so rarely
engaged with teenagers, growling
out my full name, first,
middle, last. A crow

to sit across the interminable
desk and recall all the ways
I have failed you. Always
surrounded by pictures
of inflamed and dripping
colons, slick intestines. Here

I learned to navigate
the coiled GI tract, your
unreadable scrawl. Often
I snuck in here to touch
the strict frames of each diploma. Shake
delicate vials of ink, dial buttons
on the phone. There are no photos

of me here. I am not
solemn or cerebral enough
for this space, so male and leathered
in-ornate and defined. Still

I creep in while you sleep to sit
in your tufted chair and press
my toes on the polished desk.

Oak Bay
Victoria

the ocean tosses gently, the boats
in their slips. Mannish, silent, an early sun
shoos the gauze from the water's surface. We pull
ourselves awake. I break

a dark scab on my wrist and lick
the wound, an old blood-lust. Habit,
how intimate our tongues
with our own blood.

This place
never stills. I remember
the crippling new pain
of my menstrual cycle when first I came
to the island, so near to the tide. It felt
as if my body was rushing
to give its blood back
with each lunar pull.

This morning
people are sleeping
in their boats, still drunk

from last night, rocking
in the early tide
restless, thinking
themselves still.

is this the beginning

Opal moon, sprawling
sky. Coyote yelp, magpie's
sharp cry. The elegance
of a red-winged blackbird alone

on an electric wire. The hummingbird,
its frantic thrum. Unfolding,
refolding view, glossed scallops
in the morning tide, translucent green
of pacific kelp elaborated
across stone beaches.

A woman's laughter pitched
against morning's still.

this mourning
Aunty Util

This evening the ancestors
are beating their drums, or perhaps
for you, the panmen are playing.

You have gone
to the family place
and someone is pounding
a great steel drum.
Leotha's first born child. Held
naked above the heads
of the nurses, offered up
to a bold island sky, and pressed
to your father's wide palm. Tonight,

my father is learning to mourn, a skill
he will never master. He speaks
of you gently, in a language closed
and unreaching. The family
secrets are safe, with you now.

white

white, this love
this marriage
   white   sour cream white
sheened   dewy and animal
    like sweat   the frozen fat cream
that lifts, tips   the caps on milk bottles left
on the doorstep in winter.

White as clean as her black hair
against the white pantsuit   laced gloves
nestled in his thick brown hands
cupped lilies swaying in glass vases
spray of baby's breath in a black button hole
so white this white, she wanted
to press the flat of her tongue
to it and taste.   Lick it
like frost on the window   this love
this white love.

Then came the three girls. Then the years
of cigarette smoking
when they refused to stop
using the lightbulbs
to melt their wax crayons   refused
to stop eating
the good baker's chocolate.

It was then she could press her
fingertips to the white,
see the oiled skin spirals on it   white
a dropped petal in the palm
a curl of paint on the once-new walls.

It was then the dull ochre of scalded milk,
whiskey and cream in the coffee

on Christmas morning.   That taste
of Eucharist mixed with tequila
from the night before.

This white, slowly yellowed cream
tired colour of breath
and steam from showers and the fumes
from hair relaxers. Beef curry
she burned and he ate anyway
complaining the whole evening
of a stomach ache. It was the colour of her belly
getting fatter and rippled   the rope of scar
from her   last pregnancy. The colour
of book pages too long
unread. The colour
of an unclean refrigerator door.

In the end, it was a beach stone   dull
and pebbled. Paint peeling on the garage
and a man who couldn't even use a hand sander.
His suitcase sitting at the end
of the stairwell. And their girls a braided line
hearing him say how he hates to leave them.

She recalls how she worked
at the folding of towels
at the kneading of bread dough
the kicking off of graveled snow
from the undercarriage
of the car but in the end   what she had
was the colour
of the once-white wedding sheets
after seventeen years
washed and still
slept upon.

Autumn
Letitia-Elizabeth

How beautiful the earth
is these mornings, preparing
itself for sleep. As winter quills
softly in, the leaves
a restless fall. The colourless sky

swells with snow and fat rain
then voids itself. And you, my stormy
fawn-eyed niece, you watch
the webbing in of frost
on the wooden frame, lick
your slender finger and write
on the glass, your name,

a face, dotted eyes and
a frown. You have always been
a sad and heavy child, shunning back
the closeness of your adult time. You catch me

in your lonesome reflection and I am ashamed
to have given myself up
so easily.

How beautiful you are, my girl.

one last portrait

Breath spirals ahead
in this thick and heavy air. Behind me
you trail on the loose scrabble
of a grey and sandless beach. The wind
lifts my skirt again
and again. Behind me, you

capture the beach, defog
your stubborn lens cap
with a damp fleece sleeve. Again
and again the wet air

creeps in and dews, dripping
from our slacked mouths, swallowing
everything; the you, the me. Here,
there is no birdsong, lapped shore
no insect hovering
above curled water. Now and again

a scattering sound: stones
as you approach.

the girl considers the rainbow
for Ntozake Shange

Did I consider the rainbow? Not the rainbow,
nor suicide, nor the wide back
                    of a man walking away
with all my stuff in tow. Yes,
        my stuff, all. Did I consider
the rainbow?   Or the mellow song
        of a single girl, a man who smiled
a little too long, coy-dogged his way in then
                    palmed my stuff
into his cracked paw like mud? No

not rainbows,   nor suicide,
        nor yellow half-black girls,
but *retail*. The rag bin, marked down, priced
to clear. Slashed. That
        'what can I get with what I got?
The change that slips
        between the sofa cushions.
A creased brown bag, wet at the mouth.

Should have been the rainbow
yes   yet
there it went.   All my stuff

like you said.

Was it the rainbow
        I considered? Again
  and again that virgin
hair, that kitchen curl
        which hedges the neck, which
never grows and constantly betrays

the flat and shining
        locks that swing above it.   See, he looked
a little too long and I thought, nice
to be looked at

at all. It's true, I was *that* girl,
        more   than   once   and the deal
seemed fair. Half-off   half-full   half-black girl

ten scarlet toenails,
        a thousand tea-coloured freckles   plucked
like Saskatoons then sucked
        of sweetness and handed
over, handful   after wet handful.   Was it

the rainbow
        I considered,

or just a place for the crooked bones
of the face to rest, for the dull cut
of male shoulder blades. Two ears

with the Willie Nelson song
        always playing   always   two chipped
and crooked front teeth, the scar
        from a fever blister under the bottom
lip, and as a bonus for shopping,   each breast
        well over a handful
a piece. Packed in,

rolled up in a careful
        row. The rainbow? Suicide?
Neither was she bitch, nor simple.   Just a little cold   perhaps
Tired   yes. Consider the rainbow?

Neither the rainbow   nor suicide, nor
a now fingerless woman

who can not dial a phone or rub the sleep
from her eyes. Just me
carried away
        in a discount bag, jangling
and tucked tight
                under a work-roughed elbow
airless
    and heavy
        and worth
                less.

22

breathless, nest of damp
hair tangling into the pale
carpet. Scissors
in a startled grip, half
open, stuck
like a bird's mouth
waiting.

She cuts back
her father's voice
we always thought
natural hair
just looked messy
chemical burns
on her eight year old
scalp, how she longed
for a ponytail
that moved when she ran.
How she longed
for the hotcomb, its burn
on her forehead. She cut

with kitchen sheers
angry clumps, her skull
getting lighter, neck
goosing straight
and graced, free
from the noose
of glossed braids. Cut

to the stem of perm
those small tufts of curl
kinked at summer's
first hot breath. how it
bounced, bushed
and stubby, revealing
a scalp, uncombed
helix, earlobe, and finally
a face.

three degrees of freedom

the largest of the human joints, femoral cup rotates then rests, the
yogis say this is the storehouse of our emotions, burdened
and stiffened by sorrow, the lost apologies. The day I left
my mother's house for my father's, a betrayal so raw I scratched
at my guilt until my fingernails bled. The day, years before,
when my father stood in the doorway, unmanned and leaving.
His face comes to mind in king pigeon pose, my weight punishing
the socket. Mechanics of movement, fingertips and floor, the bony top
of one foot, sole of the other, forehead pressed into the fists. My first love
how we ended. the wide, rollicking ferry where I sobbed so loudly
people changed their seats. Half-moon pose, breath into the hips,
pulling the muscles up and out, a rope of tissue wet with blood. Here,
I think of everyone I have ever lost. Three degrees of freedom, inferior
to the iliac crest, trochanter, poetic foot, retention of balance, tree pose
synovial, like syntax, goddess squat, birthplace. My grandmother,
braced for labour eleven times. My mother, mourning one and then
the second, as pregnancy came then left her empty. Interior rotation,
a shift on a bus bench. Exterior rotation, how we move our hips
at Carnival, wine fed by the deep artery of the thigh. The birth
of my niece, how she sucked her new skin, how similar she was
to our grandfather then, his blood showing blue and slow.

slough, scrub

the moulting of scales
on the red rat snake as it abandons
its shell in the gravel pit.

how winter creeps
in from spring, the snow
exposing grass, iris blossoms flinging
pollen through wintered lawns.

mornings, the cat sharks
to the bathroom to drink
from the broken faucet, then
reappears on the bed sheets, silent
damp, and unassuming.

nishiyuu — the people
Idle No More

snowshoes' trench, a graceful
crest across the tundra, mark
of wood and leather
a crystalline bank, upward
bite of frost on skin
seven young faces pinked
with cold, toques frozen
on downed heads. snow,

when it meets the afternoon
sun, blinds. Theirs,

the oldest voices
of the families, slow moving
and certain as caribou
letting the bones
lead, a walk
that only the young
could make.

I have never loved anything
enough.

shavasana

Still as a closed door, imagining
you above me, a cobra bending up
from your belly-button. Had
the sweat from your shoulders
dripped on me,

I would have drunk, taken
you on my tongue like rain.

Some days I still find you

on my clothing, a curve
of fair eyelash, bright
on the red wool of my coat.

I wonder if you ever pull
a twine of my hair between
your thumb and finger, a lone
ringlet tangled into the weave
of your chesterfield. If so,

forgive my presence.
I have never been good
at retreat.

blue but not in colour

august was a month with a mischievous moon, blue
but not in colour

it's true I have never been a mother, never a woman
loved

shame, how we human the wondrous things around us,
a driverless truck crashes into the stairs

today I bathed myself in smoke, sage harvested
from a tick-laden hillside

I have learned to speak a poor Michif
to the fawned brows of my sisters' sleeping children

those nights surrounding the blue moon, my body
ached, womb fisted in and anxious

some days I think it could be nice to be a mother,
to be as good a woman as my grandmother

many nights I have bloodied myself, wiped
my fingernails in the thirsty ground

it's true we were sad as children
and lonesome.

end

a barn swallow
in a closed fist.

el camino

Ah, the cadence of palms
as they move about, slow
and restless as the prairie. Here,
the coati are sleeping,
sunning themselves
in the upper fronds. My father

finds reminders of his childhood
everywhere, the agouti with their blunt
nose and deer legs, mouse ears
which twitch when the baby makes kissing
sounds at them. Perhaps I know him. Here,
in a place his bones understand.

Falling

and what of snow? how it quilts the ground, makes the spruce
bow. how gently it comes, silently building, always building,
leaving

its imprint on the garden flowers, late squash. how it fights back
the crocus, who boasts-in spring, whether the snow is ready for
sleeping. how human we become in it, ducking into our pulled
hoods, shedding our gaze from its delicate burn. how it vampires
our body warmth, sucking itself back into rain. how it settles on
our face like tears. and oh, the folly of snowploughs shovelling
the drive, moving its bulk to the banks while it stubbornly coats
back the path we've cleared. we watch it creep for weeks down
the mountain, pulling green to white until the morning we awake
and see that our lawn and truck, and the bike left slumped on the
walkway are no more

it presses the branches back to the earth

it begins

the inward curl of drying leaves
the sudden flick of silverfish
on the bathroom floor, so soft
they are a powder
underfoot. tonight

my grandfather lies restless
his ribs bruised from a fall. he has become
sleepless and confused
kicking back from his bed, talking low
and chuckling.

my mother whispers that he is talking
to my grandmother, two years
dead. I press my mouth to an old photo
of her and speak her away from his side.

pull back, I say. we are not ready.
or, if you must, take him quickly. it is the end
of autumn and the frost is making its way
through the spindled trees.

the sky is greying,
the year is in its youth.

love, selfishly

from the sky place,

through my window. Mabel,
my grandmother
asleep fifty years, and beside
her, older still, *Kahkâkô*
the Raven. Wider is the window
as they enter. The grannies
are all here tonight for me,

bîbisîs, the granddaughter. I am
the one they have been
watching. They think
my bones have all grown

wrong. Raven says,
"If she were a bird, her bones
would bend backward." "Yes,"

says Mabel, "but she is a woman.
Not a bird and these bones
have never bent backward."

Cheups, from the sideline. "Why
yuh speak so, blackbird? Dis bol-face chile
been wile all she life, buh wait nuh —
Bird? Nuh bird. De problem ear, is dis chile
dun no wear she come from. She cyah lissen."

Mabel remembers them back
to the night
I walked blind-drunk
into the sofa leg, that night
my third toe splintered,
but did not bend. *Cheups*.

Years they have been
sleeping, and still
they know my bones.

While I sleep, they run
fingers and feathers
along the molars
of my spine, keyed
ribs, they press

into the tangle, tibula,
femur, ulna, radius
the mapped cracks
of a fractured
ankle, a locked jaw. Puzzle

me back. "Empty,"
says Raven, "But she is not
a bird." They enter
the rusted gate
of my sternum. "Eh eh."

"Jus blood."
"A heart and lungs."
"It's no wonder
she does not grow."

They tell
their stories into the web
of blood. *Kahkâkô* sings
with his remembering tongue
and the grannies
beat their many drums. They fill

the space: metacarpal, deer skin
drum, metatarsal, steel pan,
blunt roots, incisor, all the places
where young bones
meet. Weave pelvis
and thigh, rib rib rib
radial nerve bundle, the spot
which opens the hand. I sink
into the mattress' nest, body
fighting, breath.

"It will hurt," says Raven.
Mabel says, "It always does."
Cheups.

Albért, Laura

and Laurél, who came after

My great-grandfather, knees deep
in the alfalfa, dark suspenders bowed
along his chest. A man not easily wearied,
his jaw the sturdy curve supporting
a bridge. Pressed shirt tucked
into his waistband.

His black hair is parted sharply to the left,
his head tilted in the same direction as
·if to regard my fingertips.

The striped tie is too short for a man
of his width and brawn. Men like Albért
would only wear a tie to a funeral
or special occasion. Beside him

is Laura, her dress wrinkled
in the prairie wind. Laura, fat
and bellied. She does not smile

but squints. Maybe
she longed for a dress
the colour of spring beets, some
nylon stockings, enough flour
for a Saskatoon pie, a ripe orange. She tucks

her hands behind her back to hide
the crooked edges of her fingernails,
the legacy of carbolic soap from the laundry
scrubbed out back, the stink of cabbage
and corned beef rising from her skin and hair.

Now and again, I smell the photo's surface,
smell Colonsay, its wet crops and turned soil.

At Laura's waist is small Maríe
in her First Communion dress. Maríe
will have a sister soon. She peeks
out from the folds in her mother's skirt, silly
in her white flowered dress and veil. Freckled
hands clasped before her, knee socks
sagging on narrow calves, Maríe
must have liked the camera.
Beside her mother's hip
she smiles.

roti, chicken thigh, garlic, and rum

This, our oldest story. My mother's recipe, carried back to her
place of lengthy winter and edgeless sky in a notebook rough
with turmeric and flour. Tonight my sister's child is licking dahl
from a wooden spoon. She has six small teeth, yellowed
with spice. My mother claps the flour from her palms

Hers is a clean and modern kitchen, bright and wide and cool.
She greases her knuckles with lard, pinches thyme
from the stem, sniffs her thumbnail and tells us, again,
of her time in Port of Spain, how she arrived white and young
and newly wed, her passport inked with a single stamp. Bumpkin,
she says fondly, embarrassingly Catholic, painfully shy. How the heat
slammed into her and coated her skin like spit. Split

pea, sea salt, the small white seeds from bird peppers. I know
this method as my tongue knows my teeth. Each ingredient,
invokes Leotha the long dead mother-in-law, her smell of sweat
and palmade. In her housecoat pocket, a tonic of rum
and full cloves of garlic and pepper. My father, fresh
from medical school. Leotha's bush remedies,
his old life, the kitchen dark and small. In the back of the house,
how the stove's heat settled against the stucco bringing the walls
and ceiling in. How she sweated.

How the house was full of lizards and flying roaches when the lights
went out. There was a mango tree, she says suddenly,
wistfully. Right there in the yard. She presses
the rolling pin. As a child, I sat on the counter as she worked.
As a woman, I strip the skin and bones from the chicken. She huffs
as I sneak coconut milk into the curry, thinking myself smarter. Tonight,

my cousins will smell it in the stew and refuse to eat it. Piling
their plates instead with my mother's rice and pigeon peas,
and the empty roti skins. My mother's other eye
on the hot oiled pan. The only prize from her first
marriage, her one grand adventure, her biggest mistake. The baby
claps her hands as my mother flips the skins and pulls them from
the pan just before they burn. When the skins are cooled, she folds
them into a damp white towel. They are soft and freckled,
like us.

Trinidad, 1957

Entrance Exam
Queen's Royal College

Four AM, the boy muffles
the electric alarm he keeps
beneath his pillow. In the dark room,
his older siblings sleep tangled. The baby,
Dennis, six-years-old, sleeps
with their mother still. Their father, Milton,
is dead five years. The eldest boy, Andrew,

is nearly grown, restless
for Canada. The boy sleeps
each night above
his ticking clock, time breaching
the shortest sleep. He is ten-
years-old and already his sisters
have begun to marry.

He wakes, creeps into
the kitchen to mark
out his sums. One thing
he knows, above all else,
he does not want to be
a mechanic. Can not be. He scratches
the yellow sleep
from his eye. He has learned
the names of each island
in order, labels again,
their perfect arch
on the blue Caribbean sea. Writes

sedimentary and sand, mountainous
and jungle. Maps each region, imagines
himself grown, oil stains
on dull coveralls. He can not be
a mechanic, and so he does
his sums. At school
he has learned to make
no mistakes, to never speak
out, to commit to his mind each line
of Shakespeare.

In secret, he loves
Sherlock Holmes but the Hound
of Dartmoor
will have to wait. He studies
until the house comes awake. Today

he is scrubbed, uniform
pressed. His mother slips
a few dear coins into his pocket, their weight
new in the lining. She does not remind
him how important today is but instead
rubs a brush roughly on his hair and wordlessly
tugs his collar straight.

Andrew, drives him to town. He will
make his own way
home.

Strange, the school's stillness. Cricket
bats dashed on the pitch, the hallways
windless and heavy. There are only two
from his village here. All strive, but the prize

is not for all. Thirty thousand boys, to be pressed
into ninety narrow spaces. He feels the engine
grease under his trimmed fingernails. These halls
have fallen motionless, save for
this frantic penning of facts.

Afterwards, he finds
a diner with a stretched and polished
counter, pulls himself up
on a high bar stool. He has been
to the city before, but never
on his own. This is the first
meal he has eaten

in a restaurant. He orders
a cheese sandwich and
peanut punch. Eats hungrily, sleep
creeping back from months of study. This,
the nicest meal he has ever tasted. He swings
his feet high, above the well-swept floor.

Little grandchile gull, why yuh judge me so?

Leotha Morgan

Yuh say dat if me beat yuh fadder
less, if me hug he
and hole he, maybe den
he'd ah love
yuh bedda. Dat dis
my doin, de way
he love yuh now.

Yuh tink, every ting
won bin differen
if me leh dose wil' boys ah mine
run round Port ah Spain like dem
have no sense in dey head,
lime in de street
like a pack a ragamuffin teef
got nuh brought-up-sy?

Yuh ain't got no husban. Yuh
nuh no me, chile.

Yuh never had tuh skin
an bleed de chicken
wile yuh fat pregnant
got babies wailin
and husban steppin
out, makin style wit de women
in town. Yuh no dis,
you'd have trown
dem flower pot too, aim
at he well shine shoes.

Yuh never had babies coming one
an den nex
an den nex
til de house stuff wit babies
eight mouts beggin' food
and a husban gone. Yuh dun know
dis story, chile. Yuh cyah say.

So me nuh gun tell yuh,
me shud ha hug
yuh fadder more
me shud bin softer
wit dem children ah me own.

Never dun no chile
no good bein hug, yah no dis.
huggin' dem chilren
nuh put food in dey belly. No
shut on dey back.

So tuck dat chin down, little gyal chile.
Yuh nuh no me. Yuh nuh no dis
story. Me tell yuh dis:
huggin' dem chilren
won been nuttin
but huggin'.

as much a beginning as any
Humboldt

The old train station. So many of the stories start
in places like this. Our bones are the iron and weed
of this province, dry and endless. Strapped
always to the horizon, moving always
moving. Here, I feel

my skin unpeel, expose its wet
under-pinning, the tangle of muscle, silk
of the inner cheek. This, the railway
our mothers played on as children, the line
where our grandfather sweated, puked
his whiskey behind the switch house, then
rinsed his mouth and reported, always,
to work. Of course, the rails are silent
now, and the switch house
boarded. This railway which stamped
itself across the plains swathing through farm
and scrip, returns to the earth
as well. We walk to the old family home

its screened in porch where Aunty Shelley
slept, a tumour eating
her ten-year-old brain. Our uncle
and his twin were nine that autumn.
He remembers this and boyishly kicks
at the asphalt. He remembers
how they buried their grandmother
months later in the Protestant cemetery.

Together, we look
for Shelley's tombstone, finding only
a small wooden cross, her name and age
in careful white paint.

This is the place. Here,
our family was
put to seed.

Mabel

for the baby, Mabel

I had that name once. Monkman, the family
name. Mother was Maggie, a midwife
who delivered the Indian babies
on the Halcro reservation. Father
was James. They were married
fifty-eight years. I had a sister
called Sahra, an uncommon
name. Never was it pronounced right,
never spelled correctly. Sarha,
my eldest sister. And I, Mabel.

My hair greyed after
my sixteenth birthday and I feared
I would never be beautiful. I cut
it short, wore it just below my earlobes. Always
was I skinny and tall, every joint
angled and sharp. Corners and rails. I never smiled
when my photo was taken. When I married, I left
the reservation and never
returned. He was Ted, mischief and kind, chased

from Ireland by a stern and lawful
family. He was broad
but was not tall, his jeans
cuffed at the ankle to keep them
from dragging in the mud. He made his way
to Canada, out of his father's view, and married
an Indian girl. Though
after that day, I was Indian
no more. My children, Irish. They were gifted
their father's name.

A plume of noise and fists
and legs were my children, four
as wild as night. My girl,
Norah, wildest of all, blessed
with her father's good humour
and her mother's bad temper. I put them out
in the yard to cool off, even in winter. Bolted the door
on them, every one.

My boys, I gave to the war. What a time
that was for mothers.
They volunteered for the promise
of work, said they wanted to see
the world outside St. Louis. So proud
were they in their army greens
when I kissed them, each goodbye.

Three I gave. Two returned.
They worked the rails, married,
had babies. Came home
as promised, but my youngest boy Reg
he never came back. Survived
the war, then vanished. Leaving me
with a single photo of us, stood on the porch
on the day he shipped off. Lifetimes
later, they would find him again, living
hard on the streets of Vancouver,
stubborn as a wolfpup. By then
I was a long time gone, and had never
wept for the relief of finding him. My youngest.
Never did we mourn him well.

The last thing I did as a mother
was to watch my boy John
bury his little girl. That was the last year
of my life. I sat at his kitchen table,
a bowl of sour cream and brown sugar
growing warm in front of me, and watched
him staring his grief
into a cup of strong black coffee.
I did not go to him. Perhaps,

the only comfort
I had left me
the day my youngest boy
did not come home.

I had nothing to give and so I watched.

They buried me
in Autumn, and I went
to the grasses, returned
to my mother and her people.

Shook off my Irish name
and remembered the name
of my bones. Monkman. Still was I
skinny and grey haired, angles and corners
and rails. Mother,
grandmother, widow.

Unsmiling,
quiet as a quail.

Layla

She sits breached in my sister's womb, kicking
out her new feet, soles pressing back
through layers of muscle and skin. Barefoot
and wild, already we know

she is ours. Frantic, she is her auntie's
child, mine, born first after our grandmother
walked on. She does not know
the stories. Her feet will never be
washed and kissed
in the ways we remember. And yet

she kicks out her place, ghosting the dead
in her watered ears, the rapid heart, papered
skin, tiny fists. They whisper their names
in Michif and French, the old tongues. Charlotte,
Sofia, Mabel, Laurél. Systolic rhythm
of drum and beach, canoes breaking
in rivers, ploughs in flattened earth. They sing
her into this family, telling her
kick, kick, kick.

Split Pea Soup

Field peas on pink formica. Peas the colour
of unrefined wheat, the stems
of dead impatiens. They use a wet lace
tablecloth to gather them. She adds salt
to the stockpot, tap water, a drop of oil.

Farmsoil gives them a fine grey dusting
which smells of runoff
from the plywood mill. It fed
her sisters as children, then robbed
their young wombs, leaving bloody
handfuls of fetus, ladled
from toilets, banks of snow.

Her stepfather's palms spread on the field peas,
mechanic's hands, residue of work in the ridges
of his thumbs, the surface of his rough
and tidy fingernails. Knees crack
and pop barely able to carry
stiff legs, waist, shoulders, head
from table to yellow stove and back again.

He was a young man in this town, riding
a bicycle backward down the unsloping road
his view the back tire rolling, retreating
asphalt, his arms pressing handlebars
behind his now crooked back. Nowadays
his bicycle rusts in the quonset. Flypaper swings

in the window, tempting flies
and yellow-jackets. An open screen drawing
in mill-smell, mould mossing

the rippled linoleum and baseboards,
shitkickers askew in the doorway.

They sift out sharp twigs, clumps
of knotted dirt and grass, shrivelled
husks of beetles and spiders. Funnel
the peas into a large metal sieve, run
them under the tap, gravel and grainy
mud scraping the steel kitchen sink.

In the tap water, the peas drop
like quartz. The rotten ones float
like soap bubbles and the step-father
fishes them out with a wet wooden spoon.

When she was little, this was the spoon
he spanked her with wide and flat. They add to the water
before turning on the heat, rosemary,
sage, and a hambone, bloody.

love poem

Fat raven in a swaying poplar outside my bedroom window.
Nest of black babies, mouths open.

Your skin, the colour of soil runnelled with rainwater
seeking underground streams. My fantasy fingers

tangled in around your heavy dreadlocks. Pregnant
dew hanging from pink camellias. I drink it.

The cuticles of your index fingers wet with spit,
chewed skin bled pink on your full bottom lip.

My open palms shiny with hair oil,
I lick them and they taste unclean

like you.

Trinidad, 1997

My father pays a man for a coconut from his cart,
offers it to me and tooths a smile.

It's heavier than I expected
and deep, fleshy green.

The floral juices perfume my skin
as it spills from my mouth. We walk

through narrow, shadowed streets,
our shoulders nearly

touching in the humidity. This,
the closest we've ever been.

Even his accent is different here.
It rushes his tongue, removes

the vestigial prairie
reawakens a time before the long dark winters.

Old neighbours wave in the heat, appearing
from dark stucco houses, pink curlers

in greased hair peeking
from plastic shower caps, women

with toothbrushes dangling
from slackened mouths, thin hands

on the inward sway of their backs.
They call my father, "Earlie."

green banana

Trinidad

My father rubs his palm on a banana tree, ducks
between them one by one, dodging things slow-
moving yet unseen. Speaks of how to keep a grove
in fruit. Ours, he says, was small: four squat trees
their tubers swinging narrow
on the stalk, flower a deep bruise, its lick

of red. The fruits fan and then drop, exhausting
back to the grove. He presses his thumbnail
to the trunk and it weeps a slow, guava
coloured frown. He says,

Green banana is bitter, it furs the tongue
and the back of the teeth, brings thickness
to the mouth. It is best when cooked
long, in stew. His mother's fish broth
simmered low, heads of snapper bobbing
from the cast iron pot.

If you eat it raw, he says,
it will ruin you.

daughter

She is her mother's daughter, closed
as a punched eye. Spinster, too long
on the shelf. She knows
she will never be
happy. At night,

she stares into the mirror, raking
braids into her scalp, the nerves
long dead from her mother's
impatient hand. As closed

as a punched eye, she pulls roughly
at the hair as her mother did, trying
always to quiet her wild.

To our mothers
we are a very old joy
an old misery.

rib of Adam

She clings like a starved fox
her swallowed fear, the frosting over
of pavement too early in autumn, fittingness
of winter after the fall. How my sisters loved
the end of summer, and all the ways
we have learned to mourn. Us, our vaginal grace

the old bones of Eve, canoed
ribs, rapidity of cells. Her dark
eye socket a tunnelled hive
of blood and nerve. We married her
beauty long lives ago. First Woman

Wise Woman. Grandmother,
the bitch coyote, big lipped, curved
rough heels stamped
into sand. This, the elegy
we sing as we exit our mothers.

The last snow of spring
the cow leaving the barn
for the pasture. The farmer, stalking
her, bringing her stubborn, swollen body
back to the safely lit barn where
her calf will be born braying, licked

clean, moved
from the barn to the mudroom
for warmth. How there, the calf will cry
through the porch screen
for its mother, milk-heavy
and restless in the yard. Elegy,
the oldest womans' song.

34

skipped stones
a man hunting
flints and
pressing them
into her hand, remarking
on her fingers, how small
her palms. he watches

the surface and not
her body, quiet
except the lick
of an uncalm lake

cigarette limp
in his lip
he smokes without
speaking.

after the stones
are thrown, they drink
facing shore.
a boulder, their table.

it means nothing, this

sudden appearance of you at my door. My awkward lean
against the door frame as you stroll from the elevator.

We embrace, we always do, and I breathe
the cold-leather smell of your coat.

My eyes still reach just shy of your shoulder. Years have passed
and I have not grown. Wet leather gets my kiss.

You look at me like I am a woman. The ugliness
of youth chipped from my body. You say I look

good and my face warms as I let you in. I am still that girl, the
one
you never loved.

born at night
for Layla on her naming day

say wakomâkanak   say family   say racoon and wild
porcupine   the poplar bark curled around the fingertip
say the sound of a mother reading poems
at her eldest son's wedding say li toñeur   three little girls
under a thick quilt as the lights   flicker say lightning bug
say Grandmother   nokom   the mothering words
Charlotte Anne   say thunderbird   fiddle the perfume of sage
urned in the vestibule at church   say Mama
                    (Therese, Laurel, Leotha, Laura. Say Mabel)

Say the one whose name you walk with   le prairie   the place
we are barefoot and feral   where we thistle our feet in the soil
say the place of our bones   say stardust at the gravesite
magic   the song we sing at supper   the frosted stain of birthday
cake on the dresses of ten little girls   say coyote   say freight
train   the sound that whistles us to sleep at night say the prairie
sky   how it pressed itself into the ground
say the grandfather words

                    (John, Milton, Isaac, and Earle)   say black bear
say onk   green hummingbird   li salay   the weave of our hands
when we come together to weep   say the funeral walks   speak
them   (Shelley, and Eddie, Marîe and Marguerîte, Raymond
and Norah and Armand)   the ones we have mourned
say Patrick   the sound of the men in the kitchen   their dominos
splitting on the tabletop   say ma tawnt   ghost them
to your sleeping side   your shoulders the steps of your spine
all the places you grow from   these are the bones of our family
the cedar pouch   assumption sash   medicine bag   the telling
of stories at a long wooden table the way the bread is left to rise
the sucking of the new calves on your fingertips   how we carry

the joyful spirits of the dead in our bodies   the mapping
of bones   how they enter us and feed on the goodness there
say wakomâkanak   spotted lily   the names which line
your infant feet   speak with your spirit tongue   remembering
tongue   the old song tongue which remembers you back
to your blessing day   this welcoming day when we held you
before the living   and our moshom lit the candles
today you learned that there are stories in the palms
of those who cradle you this day we crowded in around you
the cub of a very old family   and said to the lake
and into the sleeping place in the sky   that you would come
to know this, the meaning of your name.

today

"Don't worry about me," my grandfather
says, shaming my wet
eyelashes with each ragged exhale.

he taps his hundred-year-old finger
on his bird-like chest. "I worry
about me," he states. "You, don't."

the tea cup clatters
his mouth folds in to drink it before

I can see
it has burned him.

the returning-to place

The path you are walking
is ending, and you
have walked it
so well. This is the farthest

you will carry us
and so it is time to stretch
your legs. You have earned this
barefoot moment, this
wiggling of weary toes. Yours,

the tonguing
of the space between
gum and denture. Remove
the speaker
from your silent ear.

This is your reward,
to put down the razor
and foam, let
your whiskers soften,
set aside the brush
and paste, grow

your hair
long and wild as winter.
This is the time
for wildness. Go now

Grandpa, to the returning-to
place, shake your skin
from your bones like a lake-heavy
husky. Let go
the breath and press
your calloused feet
to the frost-cold
earth. Plant yourself.

This, the last moment
our bones will touch.

st. andrew's cathedral
Victoria, BC

this is the place
where she learned to speak
freely, to pray. the balcony
creaks and sways and
dust charms the shadowed
windows. how dark and quiet
she had been.

the only ghost here
is her own.

garden (morning)

eve peels the onions, cooks them down
slow and sweet into jam, spreads
them on hot slabs of white bread.
she considers

the wastefulness of a short romance, how
time bruises the fingertips and eels
past the webbing. years gone,
the unadorned beauty of youth, pulled
raw like a skinned calf.

across the house, the cat knocks over
a stand of cardboard from the new sofa
and bolts, fur spiked and ears flat. eve stands
in the dim kitchen amid the ruckus, fingers
stinking, refusing to cry the sting

of the onions from her eye. news
from radio speakers, just another voice
in the room, a man to drink
her wine with. there is an old musk
on her skin. in the morning,

she uncurls
beneath the duvet, curves
until her spine pops softly, fingertips
cooled and smelling of body.

love, selfishly

home

I have written of eyes and skin
lips, and teeth, and cocks. Of myself
among them, clumsy, always
bruising my knees
my hips. I have written love

selfishly, wildly. Men
who marked me
with their teeth, pressed
the skin of my thigh
between their molars. Written
myself drunk
and weeping, dripping
in blood and spit, unloved
unhandled. But

your hands, work-worn
and stoney, dwarfing mine
swallowing. You rub
a rough and calloused
thumb across my bitten nail
flexing and releasing
the muscles of your palm
like a heart, like sex.

you pull my hand
to your mouth
while we drive,
never taking your eyes
from the road, the rain
you kiss the narrow
bones, thin veins,
each polished fingernail.

At home, your mouth
finds the meat
of my palm. Tonguing
the flesh,
you close your eyes